NOT YOUR AVERAGE

Christian Gratitude Journal

Not Your Average Christian Gratitude Journal by Gratitude Daily
Published by Creative Ideas Publishing

For permissions contact:
permissions@creativeideaspublishing.com

ISBN: 978-1-952016-32-5

CREATIVE IDEAS
PUBLISHING

Hi,

This gratitude journal will help you:

- Fix your eyes on Jesus with the daily bible verse or Christian quote

- Organize your thoughts before the busy world sweeps you off your feet

- Increase your gratitude (which increases contentment!)

- Intentionally turn your burdens and desires into prayers

- "Pray far"

  (This is intended for prayers outside of your circle of life. Maybe pray for Christian leaders, local schools, injustice, politics, etc.)

- Lift your spirit as you identify atleast one thing you are looking forward to that day

  (If you can't think of anything you are looking forward to that day, make sure to add something even if it is small!)

- Store God's Word in your heart as you write down the verse you are trying to memorize

  (Find what works for you. It can be the same verse for two days or two weeks.)

- Improve your life and faith by working through the 14 "special pages" designed to do on each Saturday of this 100-day journey.

[PS: Some of the things that you are thankful for today can be specific things that happened the day before.

PPS: All 14 "Challenge Pages" could be great resources to use with a potential disciple.]

XO,
Jori Outlaw

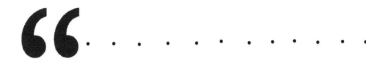

> But the Lord stood at my side
> and gave me strength.
> -2 Timothy 4:17

TODAY'S PRIORITIES:

Today, I'm thankful for:

1. ....

2. ....

3. ....

PRAYING CLOSE:

Thoughts + Dreams:

Something I'm looking forward to today is:

PRAYING FAR:

Verse

> God is able to take the mess of our past and turn it into a message. He takes the trials and tests and turns them into a testimony.
> -Christine Caine

TODAY'S PRIORITIES:

Today, I'm thankful for:

1. ....

2. ....

3. ....

PRAYING CLOSE:

Thoughts + Dreams:

Something I'm looking forward to today is:

PRAYING FAR:

Verse

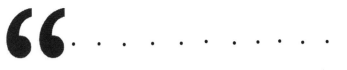

Do not conform to the pattern of this world, but be transformed by the renewing of your mind. Then you will be able to test and approve what God's will is—his good, pleasing and perfect will.
Romans 12:2

TODAY'S PRIORITIES:

Today, I'm thankful for:

1. ....

2. ....

3. ....

PRAYING CLOSE:

Thoughts + Dreams:

Something I'm looking forward to today is:

PRAYING FAR:

Verse

Never be afraid to trust an unknown future to a known God.
-Corrie ten Boom

TODAY'S PRIORITIES:

Today, I'm thankful for:

1. ....

2. ....

3. ....

PRAYING CLOSE:

Thoughts + Dreams:

Something I'm looking forward to today is:

PRAYING FAR:

Verse

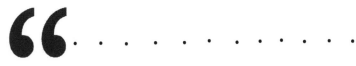

> For he has rescued us from the dominion of darkness and brought us into the kingdom of the Son he loves, in whom we have redemption, the forgiveness of sins.
> -Colossians 1:13-14

TODAY'S PRIORITIES:

Today, I'm thankful for:

1. ....

2. ....

3. ....

PRAYING CLOSE:

Thoughts + Dreams:

Something I'm looking forward to today is:

PRAYING FAR:

Verse

We are guaranteed eternal life with Jesus the moment we put our trust in Him as our Lord and Savior. *At that moment* the Holy Spirit comes and lives within us and our relationship with Jesus begins. It doesn't just start once we get to heaven. Jesus graciously walks with us through this life and wants to display Himself *to* us and *through* us every day in so many amazing ways. List some of the ways you have experienced Jesus in your life. Let's pray to experience Him more.

Here are a few examples of ways Jesus wants
to make Himself known to us in this life:

Light in the Darkness (John 8:12)   Bread of Life (John 6:35-48)

Redeemer (Ephesians 1:7, Hebrews 9:12-15)   True Vine (John 15:1-5)

Good Shepherd (John 10:11-18)   King of Kings (Revelation 17:14)

Giver of Freedom (John 8:36)   Prince of Peace (John 16:33)

Author and Perfecter of Our Faith   Surrendered to God (John 6:38, Luke
(Hebrews 12:2)   22:42)

Great High Priest Who Empathizes With Us (Hebrews 4:15-16)

I have experienced Jesus as:	It looked like this:
Example: Light in the darkness	When I went through a really hard year battling depression and grief, it felt very dark. I clung to Jesus and He was my light and strength that kept me going and kept me hopeful!

Jesus is alive

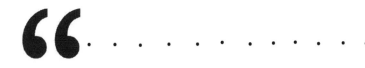

> Religion says, 'I obey; therefore I am accepted. ' Christianity says, 'I'm accepted, therefore I obey.
> -Timothy Keller

Today, I'm thankful for:

1. ....
2. ....
3. ....

PRAYING CLOSE:

Thoughts + Dreams:

Something I'm looking forward to today is:

PRAYING FAR:

Verse

". . . . .

Let us run with perseverance the race marked out for us, fixing our eyes on Jesus, the pioneer and perfecter of faith. For the joy set before him he endured the cross, scorning its shame, and sat down at the right hand of the throne of God.
-Hebrews 12:1-2

. . . . **"**

Today, I'm thankful for:

1. ....

2. ....

3. ....

PRAYING CLOSE:

Thoughts + Dreams:

Something I'm looking forward to today is:

PRAYING FAR:

Verse

"

Sometimes life is so hard you can only do the next thing. Whatever that is just do the next thing. God will meet you there.
-Elisabeth Elliot

"

Today, I'm thankful for:

1. ....

2. ....

3. ....

PRAYING CLOSE:

Thoughts + Dreams:

Something I'm looking forward to today is:

PRAYING FAR:

Verse

> But those who hope in the Lord will renew their strength. They will soar on wings like eagles; they will run and not grow weary, they will walk and not be faint.
> -Isaiah 40:31

TODAY'S PRIORITIES:

Today, I'm thankful for:

1. ....

2. ....

3. ....

PRAYING CLOSE:

Thoughts + Dreams:

Something I'm looking forward to today is:

PRAYING FAR:

Verse

> " If I find in myself a desire which no experience in this world can satisfy, the most probable explanation is that I was made for another world.
> -C.S. Lewis "

Today, I'm thankful for:

1. ....

2. ....

3. ....

PRAYING CLOSE:

Thoughts + Dreams:

Something I'm looking forward to today is:

PRAYING FAR:

Verse

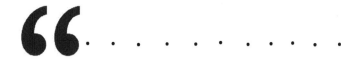

How cool is it that the same God who created oceans and mountains and galaxies thought the world needed you as well.

Today, I'm thankful for:

1. ....

2. ....

3. ....

PRAYING CLOSE:

Thoughts + Dreams:

Something I'm looking forward to today is:

PRAYING FAR:

Verse

GOD'S STORY: BIG PICTURE

3.

Redemption [Jesus came to earth to save people from the power of sin, so that their relationship with God would be redeemed. He did this by living a sinless life that we couldn't live, dying a sacrificial death on a cross that we deserved, and resurrecting from the dead proving His power and authority over all things. Through faith in His finished work on our behalf, He redeems and restores us from the inside out.]

Hebrews 9:15, Romans 3:22-26

5.

Heaven [Jesus will return for a second and final time where He will permanently bind Satan and then convert the earth into New Heaven. It will be free from sin and strife for all believers to live united with God forever.]

Acts 17:31, Revelation 21:1-27

YOUR LIFE

1.

Creation [God created the world and everything in the world and said that it was good.]

Genesis 1

2.

The Fall [Sin entered the world through Adam and Eve's rebellion and led to every person thereafter being under the power of sin.]

Genesis 3, Romans 3

4.

Decision [When you became aware of the love of God that made a way for you to be forgiven and have a personal relationship with Him through Jesus, did you believe it in faith? Was it just an intellectual agreement, a fleeting emotional experience, or was it a real and lasting heart-change where you turned away from living for yourself and now live for Christ? If the latter, then you became a new creation indwelt by the Holy Spirit, guaranteeing Heaven and all God has promised.]

2 Cor. 5:15-17, Gal. 2:20, Eph. 3:14-19, Rom. 10:9-13

The Trinity [Father God, Son Jesus, & The Holy Spirit have no beginning and no end.]

Genesis 1:2-3, John 1:1

GOD'S STORY: MY STORY

1. Is there anything holding you back from truly believing these "big picture" biblical claims to be true? Now could be a great time to ask God to help you overcome any doubt or hindrances and believe this good news by faith.

2. When you look at your life within this bigger story of God, what are your hopes for your place in it?

3. Read Matthew 22:36-39 and 2 Corinthians 5:15. What are Jesus' hopes for your life?

4. Read 1 Corinthians 10:31. Is glorifying God designed for a special time and place or are we called to glorify God in everything we do? Are there any areas in your life that maybe you didn't recognize that God wants to be apart of?

5. Sometimes we may feel like we aren't bringing God much glory because our life feels ordinary, or even mundane. But that doesn't mean that it's true! Here are some practical considerations for glorifying God in our everyday lives:

> -Am I in constant communication (prayer and worship) with God? (1 Thes. 5:16-18, John 15:4)
>
> -Am I reading His Word and meditating on it? (2 Timothy 3:16)
>
> -Am I fighting sin and pursuing righteous living? (1 John 2:1-29)
>
> -Am I pursuing Christlike love in my relationships? (John 13:34-35, 1 John 4:7-8)
>
> -Am I sharing the Good News of Jesus with others? (Colossians 4:5-6, Matthew 28:19-20)
>
> -Am I using my gifts and talents to serve others? (Romans 12, 1 Cor. 12, Eph.4, 1 Peter 4)
>
> -Am I involved with a local church? (Hebrews 10:25)

"When we trust God, He can make the ordinary extraordinary!"
-John C. Maxwell

> When there is a fight between your heart and your head, experience has taught me that the best thing you can do is pick up your Bible and remind yourself of what God says.
> -Christine Caine

TODAY'S PRIORITIES:

Today, I'm thankful for:

1. ....

2. ....

3. ....

PRAYING CLOSE:

Thoughts + Dreams:

Something I'm looking forward to today is:

PRAYING FAR:

Verse

> What comes into our mind when we think about God is the most important thing about us.
> -A.W. Tozer

TODAY'S PRIORITIES:

Today, I'm thankful for:

1. ....

2. ....

3. ....

PRAYING CLOSE:

Thoughts + Dreams:

Something I'm looking forward to today is:

PRAYING FAR:

Verse

> **"**
> And the Lord will continually guide you, and satisfy your desire in scorched places, and give strength to your bones; And you will be like a watered garden, and like a spring of water whose waters do not fail.
> -Isaiah 58:11
> **"**

TODAY'S PRIORITIES:

Today, I'm thankful for:

1. ....

2. ....

3. ....

PRAYING CLOSE:

Thoughts + Dreams:

Something I'm looking forward to today is:

PRAYING FAR:

Verse

"

I have been crucified with Christ.
It is no longer I who live, but Christ
who lives in me. And the life I now
live in the flesh I live by faith in the
Son of God, who loved me and gave
himself for me.
-Galations 2:20

"

Today, I'm thankful for:

1. ....

2. ....

3. ....

PRAYING CLOSE:

Thoughts + Dreams:

Something I'm looking
forward to today is:

PRAYING FAR:

Verse

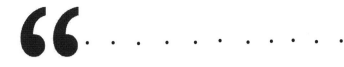

When we all reach the end of our earthly journey, we will have just begun.
-Billy Graham

Today, I'm thankful for:

1. ....

2. ....

3. ....

PRAYING CLOSE:

Thoughts + Dreams:

Something I'm looking forward to today is:

PRAYING FAR:

Verse

Be kind and compassionate to one
another, forgiving each other, just as
in Christ God forgave you.
-Ephesians 4:32

TODAY'S PRIORITIES:

Today, I'm thankful for:

1. ....

2. ....

3. ....

PRAYING CLOSE:

Thoughts + Dreams:

Something I'm looking forward to today is:

PRAYING FAR:

Verse

Discipleship Challenge

Jesus calls us to sharpen others as well as be sharpened by others.

"As iron sharpens iron, so one person sharpens another." - Proverbs 27:17

He also calls us to make disciples like He did.

"Then Jesus came to them and said, "All authority in heaven and on earth has been given to me. Therefore go and make disciples of all nations, baptizing them in the name of the Father and of the Son and of the Holy Spirit, and teaching them to obey everything I have commanded you. And surely I am with you always, to the very end of the age."
- Matthew 28:18-20

Be a Disciple

"Remember your leaders, those who spoke to you the word of God. Consider the outcome of their way of life, and imitate their faith." - Hebrews 13:7

Consider the benefits of having a mentor. You would have someone older than you who cares about you and intentionally guides you spiritually in your journey with Christ. You could confide in your mentor, ask questions to them, pray with them, and even get a close-up look at their lives. Brainstorm someone who you look up to spiritually and reach out to them asking if they would be a mentor to you. Together, you could meet once or twice a month to discuss faith and life. You could read and talk about a book of the Bible (or another helpful book), or just let your mentor choose what your time together looks like. We are never too young or too old to seek out a mentor. Pray and ask God to bring someone to mind and to give you the courage and humility to reach out.

Be a Discipler

"You then, my child, be strengthened by the grace that is in Christ Jesus, and what you have heard from me in the presence of many witnesses entrust to faithful men, who will be able to teach others also."
- 2 Timothy 2:1-2 (this describes discipleship)

Who is someone in your life with whom you have influence? What could it look like for you to love on them intentionally and help them grow in their life and faith? You could take a casual approach by inviting them into your day to day life, letting them learn from your life up close while deeper conversations naturally arise. For a more formal approach, you could reach out and ask them if they would want to meet once or twice a month to discuss faith and life with you. When you meet, you would ask them about different areas of their life and care for them. Then you could also read and talk about a book of the Bible together (or another helpful book), or just plan some verses and topics to discuss each time. The goal of biblical mentorship is to love on your mentee and care for them while also pointing them to Jesus.

In case any lies are trying to sneak in to prevent you from acting, here are some truth reminders. If you are a born-again Christian, you have the Holy Spirit in you! That makes you worthy and adequate to mentor someone else. You don't have to be perfect to mentor someone else. You simply just want to help someone else know and love Jesus more by loving and teaching them!

Possible Discipler:

Possible Disciple:

Prayer:

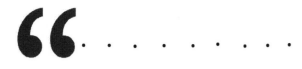

Of one thing I am perfectly
sure: God's story never ends
in ashes.
-Elisabeth Elliot

TODAY'S PRIORITIES:

Today, I'm thankful for:

1. ....

2. ....

3. ....

PRAYING CLOSE:

Thoughts + Dreams:

Something I'm looking
forward to today is:

PRAYING FAR:

Verse

For you were once darkness,
but now you are light in the
Lord. Live as children of light.
-Ephesians 5:8

TODAY'S PRIORITIES:

Today, I'm thankful for:

1. ....

2. ....

3. ....

PRAYING CLOSE:

Thoughts + Dreams:

Something I'm looking forward to today is:

PRAYING FAR:

Verse

> " The gospel is this: We are more sinful and flawed in ourselves than we ever dared believe, yet at the very same time we are more loved and accepted in Jesus Christ than we ever dared hope.
> -Timothy Keller "

TODAY'S PRIORITIES:

Today, I'm thankful for:

1. ....

2. ....

3. ....

PRAYING CLOSE:

Thoughts + Dreams:

Something I'm looking forward to today is:

PRAYING FAR:

Verse

> "
> My flesh and my heart may
> fail, but God is the strength
> of my heart and my portion
> forever.
> -Psalm 73:26
> "

TODAY'S PRIORITIES:

Today, I'm thankful for:

1. ....

2. ....

3. ....

PRAYING CLOSE:

Thoughts + Dreams:

Something I'm looking forward to today is:

PRAYING FAR:

Verse

The Son of God became a man to
enable men to become sons of God.
-C.S. Lewis

TODAY'S PRIORITIES:

Today, I'm thankful for:

1.

2.

3.

PRAYING CLOSE:

Thoughts + Dreams:

*Something I'm looking
forward to today is:*

PRAYING FAR:

Verse

Rejoice always, pray continually, give thanks in all circumstances; for this is God's will for you in Christ Jesus.
-1 Thessalonians 5:16-18

Today, I'm thankful for:

1. ....

2. ....

3. ....

PRAYING CLOSE:

Thoughts + Dreams:

Something I'm looking forward to today is:

PRAYING FAR:

Verse

Women can often name many things they wish they could change about their body. We frequently forget that God made our bodies as tools for living, not mere trophies. (Romans 12:1)

List **TWENTY** things you are thankful that your body allows you to do!

"For we are God's masterpiece. He has created us anew in Christ Jesus, so we can do the good things he planned for us long ago." – Ephesians 2:10

1.

2.

3.

4.

5.

6.

7.

8.

9.

10.

11.

12.

13.

14.

15.

16.

17.

18.

19.

20.

"For you formed my inward parts; you knitted me together in my mother's womb. I praise you, for I am fearfully and wonderfully made." – Psalm 139:14

"People look at the outward appearance, but the LORD looks at the heart." – 1 Samuel 16:7

"Do you not know that your bodies are temples of the Holy Spirit, who is in you, whom you have received from God? You are not your own; you were bought at a price. Therefore honor God with your bodies." – 1 Cor. 6:19-20

(Pray and ask God to give you strength and resources if you need to repent from harming your body in any way. Ex: undereating, overeating, obsessing, self-harm, etc.)

> If you look at the world, you'll be distressed. If you look within, you'll be depressed. But if you look at Christ, you'll be at rest.
> -Corrie ten Boom

TODAY'S PRIORITIES:

Today, I'm thankful for:

1. ....

2. ....

3. ....

PRAYING CLOSE:

Thoughts + Dreams:

{ }

Something I'm looking forward to today is:

PRAYING FAR:

Verse

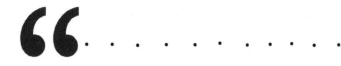

For God gave us a spirit not of fear but of power and love and self-control.
-2 Timothy 1:7

TODAY'S PRIORITIES:

Today, I'm thankful for:

1. ....

2. ....

3. ....

PRAYING CLOSE:

Thoughts + Dreams:

Something I'm looking forward to today is:

PRAYING FAR:

Verse

"

When I understand that everything happening to me is to make me more Christlike, it resolves a great deal of anxiety.
-A.W. Tozer

"

Today, I'm thankful for:

1. ....

2. ....

3. ....

PRAYING CLOSE:

Thoughts + Dreams:

Something I'm looking forward to today is:

PRAYING FAR:

Verse

> **"**
>
> Therefore if you have been raised up with Christ, keep seeking the things above, where Christ is, seated at the right hand of God. Set your mind on the things above, not on the things that are on earth.
> -Colossians 3:1-3
>
> **"**

Today, I'm thankful for:

1. ....

2. ....

3. ....

PRAYING CLOSE:

Thoughts + Dreams:

Something I'm looking forward to today is:

PRAYING FAR:

Verse

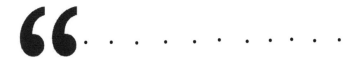

> Have I not commanded you? Be strong and courageous. Do not be afraid; do not be discouraged, for the Lord your God will be with you wherever you go.
> -Joshua 1:9

TODAY'S PRIORITIES:

Today, I'm thankful for:

1. ....

2. ....

3. ....

PRAYING CLOSE:

Thoughts + Dreams:

{ }

Something I'm looking forward to today is:

PRAYING FAR:

Verse

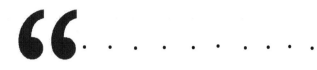

Do what you can, with what
you have, where you are.
-Theodore Roosevelt

TODAY'S PRIORITIES:

Today, I'm thankful for:

1. ....

2. ....

3. ....

PRAYING CLOSE:

Thoughts + Dreams:

*Something I'm looking
forward to today is:*

PRAYING FAR:

Verse

PHYSICAL HEALTH

Evaluate the following questions on a scale of 1 through 10 with 1 being the absolute worst and 10 being the absolute best.

How healthy is my nutrition? (Let's consider this question in terms of nutrients provided to the body, not just counting calories.)

1   2   3   4   5   6   7   8   9   10   I'm thankful for:

Some healthy foods I enjoy are:

Thoughts/Goals:

The USDA recommends eating 5-9 servings of fruit and veggies per day, how many am I eating?

1   2   3   4   5   6   7   8   9   10   I'm thankful for:

Thoughts/Goals:

How healthy is my strength and fitness?

1   2   3   4   5   6   7   8   9   10   I'm thankful for:

Thoughts/Goals:

How healthy is my body image?

1   2   3   4   5   6   7   8   9   10   I'm thankful for:

Thoughts/Goals:

How healthy is my hydration?

1   2   3   4   5   6   7   8   9   10   I'm thankful for:

Thoughts/Goals:

How well am I doing with the recommended doctor/dentist/eye visits?

1   2   3   4   5   6   7   8   9   10   I'm thankful for:

Thoughts/Goals:

Exercise is a celebration of what your body can do. Not a punishment for what you ate.

"So whether you eat or drink, or whatever you do, do it all for the glory of God." - 1 Cor. 10:3

Health is not about the weight you lose. It's about the life you gain.

> Your word is a lamp to my feet and a light to my path.
> -Psalm 119:105

TODAY'S PRIORITIES:

Today, I'm thankful for:

1. ....

2. ....

3. ....

PRAYING CLOSE:

Thoughts + Dreams:

Something I'm looking forward to today is:

PRAYING FAR:

Verse

> Whatever you do, work at it with all your heart, as working for the Lord, not for human masters, since you know that you will receive an inheritance from the Lord as a reward. It is the Lord Christ you are serving.
> -Colossians 3:23-24

TODAY'S PRIORITIES:

Today, I'm thankful for:

1. ....

2. ....

3. ....

PRAYING CLOSE:

Thoughts + Dreams:

Something I'm looking forward to today is:

PRAYING FAR:

Verse

> Consider it pure joy, my brothers and sisters, whenever you face trials of many kinds, because you know that the testing of your faith produces perseverance. Let perseverance finish its work so that you may be mature and complete, not lacking anything.
> -James 1:2-4

Today, I'm thankful for:

1. ....

2. ....

3. ....

PRAYING CLOSE:

Thoughts + Dreams:

Something I'm looking forward to today is:

PRAYING FAR:

Verse

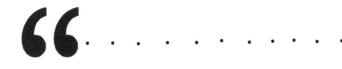

> Being a Christian is more than just an instantaneous conversion - it is a daily process whereby you grow to be more and more like Christ.
> -Billy Graham

TODAY'S PRIORITIES:

Today, I'm thankful for:

1. ....

2. ....

3. ....

PRAYING CLOSE:

Thoughts + Dreams:

Something I'm looking forward to today is:

PRAYING FAR:

Verse

Remember this: Whoever sows
sparingly will also reap sparingly,
and whoever sows generously will
also reap generously.
-2 Corinthians 9:6

Today, I'm thankful for:

1. ....

2. ....

3. ....

PRAYING CLOSE:

Thoughts + Dreams:

Something I'm looking
forward to today is:

PRAYING FAR:

Verse

> The steadfast love of the Lord never ceases; his mercies never come to an end; they are new every morning; great is your faithfulness.
> -Lamentations 3:22-23

Today, I'm thankful for:

1. ....

2. ....

3. ....

PRAYING CLOSE:

Thoughts + Dreams:

Something I'm looking forward to today is:

PRAYING FAR:

Verse

FINANCIAL HEALTH

"You must gain control over your money or the lack of it will forever control you." - Dave Ramsey

6 TIPS TO IMPROVE YOUR FINANCIAL HEALTH:

1. Spend less than you earn. This is way easier said than done, but nowadays inexpensive websites and apps (i.e. YNAB, EveryDollar) can help tremendously by providing easy-to-use budgets that even sync with your bank account. The word "budget" can make people tighten up with all sorts of negative emotions, but it's actually a tool for freedom. Poor financial health affects stress, relationships, lifestyle, and more. Budgeting simply helps you know where every dollar of your money is going.

2. Attack debt. Debt can be easily acquired, but hard to pay off. Once interest rates are tacked on and more loans get added, debt takes you further than you planned to go and hinders your life. The first step is simple: Stop taking on any kind of new debt. The second step is to prioritize paying off any current debt. For more support in this pursuit, research Dave Ramsey's "Debt Snowball Method."

3. Set aside money to give. Are we giving in a way that shows our heart is set on things above and not on earthly things (Col. 3:1-4)? Of course we should enjoy the things God gives us, but Christians are also called to give generously, not just out of obedience but out of response to God in worship. Are we passionate about giving to support those who are preaching the same gospel that changed our lives? Are we eager to share God's love and grace by helping others in need? Many people who wait to give until they have more money will still not give, because giving is a matter of the heart. Check out 2 Corinthians 9:6-15 for more encouragement on generosity.

4. Set up an emergency fund. Emergency funds ideally have three to six months (or more) of your income saved to cover unexpected hardships and expenses. Pro tip: It's helpful to separate this fund from your checking account so that it's less tempting to spend.

5. Make financial goals. Jot down a few goals you may have such as a holiday vacation, house down payment, saving or investing. Then look at your income and expenses and figure out how to achieve your goals. It may take trimming certain expenses or taking on a side hustle, but if you keep your eyes fixed on why you're sacrificing, you are more likely to make it happen.

6. Start learning about investments. Investing can seem intimidating, but it can be easily learned or guided, and it offers many benefits, most noteworthy being retirement. A great first step is to listen to an informative podcast, read an article or book, or set up a free advice call with a financial planner.

RECOMMENDED FINANCIAL RESOURCES:

- Dave Ramsey has resources across all platforms from podcasts to online articles to books and more. A great first purchase would be his best-selling book "The Total Money Makeover: A Proven Plan for Financial Fitness".

- Clark Howard and Rachel Cruze both have popular tips and resources out as well on money management.

- Etsy.com has many "financial planner printables" if you find yourself needing inexpensive and customizable tools for your financial freedom journey.

REFLECTIVE QUESTIONS:

Do you tend to be a saver or a spender? What are some advantages and disadvantages to your answer?

How does Hebrews 12:11 apply to all six tips listed above?

What are a few steps you could take to improve your financial health?

Look up "bible verses about money" and journal about some that stood out to you.

Never be lacking in zeal, but keep your spiritual fervor, serving the Lord.
-Romans 12:11

TODAY'S PRIORITIES:

Today, I'm thankful for:

1. ....

2. ....

3. ....

PRAYING CLOSE:

Thoughts + Dreams:

Something I'm looking forward to today is:

PRAYING FAR:

Verse

"

Sometimes when you're in a dark place you think you've been buried, but you've actually been planted.
-Christine Caine

TODAY'S PRIORITIES:

"

Today, I'm thankful for:

1. ....

2. ....

3. ....

PRAYING CLOSE:

Thoughts + Dreams:

Something I'm looking forward to today is:

PRAYING FAR:

Verse

> For we do not have a high priest who is unable to empathize with our weaknesses, but we have one who has been tempted in every way, just as we are—yet he did not sin. Let us then approach God's throne of grace with confidence, so that we may receive mercy and find grace to help us in our time of need.
> -Hebrews 4:15-16

Today, I'm thankful for:

1. ....

2. ....

3. ....

PRAYING CLOSE:

Thoughts + Dreams:

Something I'm looking forward to today is:

PRAYING FAR:

Verse

> To be loved but not known is comforting but superficial. To be known and not loved is our greatest fear. But to be fully known and truly loved is, well, a lot like being loved by God. It is what we need more than anything.
> -Timothy Keller

Today, I'm thankful for:

1. ....

2. ....

3. ....

PRAYING CLOSE:

Thoughts + Dreams:

Something I'm looking forward to today is:

PRAYING FAR:

Verse

> "
> When you pass through the waters, I will be with you; and when you pass through the rivers, they will not sweep over you. When you walk through the fire, you will not be burned; the flames will not set you ablaze.
> -Isaiah 43:2
> "

Today, I'm thankful for:

1. ....

2. ....

3. ....

PRAYING CLOSE:

Thoughts + Dreams:

Something I'm looking forward to today is:

PRAYING FAR:

Verse

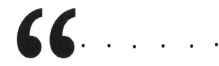

True humility is not thinking
less of yourself; it is thinking of
yourself less.
-C.S. Lewis

TODAY'S PRIORITIES:

Today, I'm thankful for:

1.

2.

3.

PRAYING CLOSE:

Thoughts + Dreams:

*Something I'm looking
forward to today is:*

PRAYING FAR:

Verse

MENTAL HEALTH

"Do not conform to the pattern of this world, but be transformed by the renewing of your mind. Then you will be able to test and approve what God's will is—his good, pleasing and perfect will." - Romans 12:2

"Take captive every thought to make it obedient to Christ." - 2 Cor. 10:5

What are 5 things that stir up positivity in you?

1.

2.

3.

4.

5.

we fall.

we break.

WE FAIL.

but

then,

WE RISE.

we heal.

WE OVERCOME.

1. Are there any negative thoughts that you tend to dwell on that you should "take captive" and stop thinking about? Try to memorize verses from God's Word that apply to those negative thoughts and then choose to dwell on God's promises and character instead. Jot down a few scripture references below that speak hope or comfort towards your struggles. (Hint: You can search the internet for some)

2. What are some things in your life that tend to cause negativity in you?

3. Are there any steps you could take towards elimination of those things?

4. What are some habits that might could improve your mental health?
(e.g., daily walks outside, 5-minute deep breathing exercises, Christ-centered biblical counseling, healthy boundaries in commitments, screen time, etc.)

> " The Lord is my shepherd; I shall not want. He makes me lie down in green pastures. He leads me beside still waters. He restores my soul. He leads me in paths of righteousness for his name's sake. Even though I walk through the valley of the shadow of death, I will fear no evil, for you are with me. "
> -Psalm 23:1-4

TODAY'S PRIORITIES:

Today, I'm thankful for:

1. ....

2. ....

3. ....

PRAYING CLOSE:

Thoughts + Dreams:

Something I'm looking forward to today is:

PRAYING FAR:

Verse

" . . . .

How completely satisfying to turn
from our limitations to a God that
has none.
–A.W. Tozer.

. . . . **"**

Today, I'm thankful for:

1. ....

2. ....

3. ....

PRAYING CLOSE:

Thoughts + Dreams:

*Something I'm looking
forward to today is:*

PRAYING FAR:

Verse

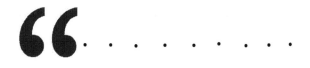

He gives strength to the
weary and increases the
power of the weak.
-Isaiah 40:29

TODAY'S PRIORITIES:

Today, I'm thankful for:

1. ....

2. ....

3. ....

PRAYING CLOSE:

Thoughts + Dreams:

*Something I'm looking
forward to today is:*

PRAYING FAR:

Verse

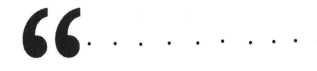

What wings are to a bird and sails to a ship, so is prayer to the soul.
-Corrie ten Boom

TODAY'S PRIORITIES:

Today, I'm thankful for:

1. ....
2. ....
3. ....

PRAYING CLOSE:

Thoughts + Dreams:

Something I'm looking forward to today is:

PRAYING FAR:

Verse

For we are God's handiwork, created in Christ Jesus to do good works, which God prepared in advance for us to do.
-Ephesians 2:10

TODAY'S PRIORITIES:

Today, I'm thankful for:

1. ....

2. ....

3. ....

PRAYING CLOSE:

Thoughts + Dreams:

Something I'm looking forward to today is:

PRAYING FAR:

Verse

> God has infinite attention to spare for each one of us. You are as much alone with him as if you were the only being he had ever created.
> -C.S. Lewis

TODAY'S PRIORITIES:

Today, I'm thankful for:

1. ....

2. ....

3. ....

PRAYING CLOSE:

Thoughts + Dreams:

Something I'm looking forward to today is:

PRAYING FAR:

Verse

Genesis 50:20 is such a treasure to read. After we see Joseph envied by his brothers, sold by them into slavery, falsely accused and then imprisoned, we then see how God uses Pharaoh to honor and promote him to second-in-command of all of Egypt! Joseph says, "You intended to harm me, but God intended it for good to accomplish what is now being done, the saving of many lives."

● ● ● ●

"And we know that in all things God works for the good of those who love him, who have been called according to his purpose."

Romans 8:28

Write about a time or two when God brought good out of a hard situation.

> " One thing I ask of the Lord, this is what I seek: that I may dwell in the house of the Lord all the days of my life, to gaze upon the beauty of the Lord and to seek him in his temple.
> -Psalm 27:4 "

Today, I'm thankful for:

1. ....

2. ....

3. ....

PRAYING CLOSE:

Thoughts + Dreams:

Something I'm looking forward to today is:

PRAYING FAR:

Verse

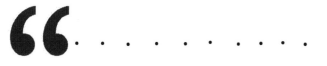

For it is by grace you have been saved, through faith—and this is not from yourselves, it is the gift of God— not by works, so that no one can boast
-Ephesians 2:8-9

TODAY'S PRIORITIES:

Today, I'm thankful for:

1. ....

2. ....

3. ....

PRAYING CLOSE:

Thoughts + Dreams:

Something I'm looking forward to today is:

PRAYING FAR:

Verse

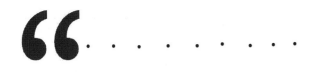

> Worry does not empty tomorrow of its sorrow; it empties today of its strength.
> -Corrie ten Boom

TODAY'S PRIORITIES:

Today, I'm thankful for:

1. ....

2. ....

3. ....

PRAYING CLOSE:

Thoughts + Dreams:

Something I'm looking forward to today is:

PRAYING FAR:

Verse

Kind words are like honey–
sweet to the soul and healthy
for the body.
-Proverbs 16:24

TODAY'S PRIORITIES:

Today, I'm thankful for:

1. ....

2. ....

3. ....

PRAYING CLOSE:

Thoughts + Dreams:

Something I'm looking forward to today is:

PRAYING FAR:

Verse

"

Don't dig up in doubt, what
you planted in faith.
-Elisabeth Elliot

"

Today, I'm thankful for:

1. ....

2. ....

3. ....

PRAYING CLOSE:

Thoughts + Dreams:

*Something I'm looking
forward to today is:*

PRAYING FAR:

Verse

> Do not be anxious about anything, but in every situation, by prayer and petition, with thanksgiving, present your requests to God. And the peace of God, which transcends all understanding, will guard your hearts and your minds in Christ Jesus.
> -Philippians 4:6-7

TODAY'S PRIORITIES:

Today, I'm thankful for:

1. ....

2. ....

3. ....

PRAYING CLOSE:

Thoughts + Dreams:

Something I'm looking forward to today is:

PRAYING FAR:

Verse

A.C.T.S PRAYER TOOL	EXAMPLES	PRACTICE
Adoration: Worship God for who He is, what He's done, and what He promises to do. 1 Chronicles 16:8-34, Rev. 4:2-8	Creator, King, Savior, Holy, Faithful, Trustworthy, Good, Patient, Loving, Just, Merciful, Compassionate, Omnipresent, Omnipotent, Healer, Omniscient, Forgiving, Prince of Peace, Gracious, Provider, Our Strength, Emmanuel, etc.	God, I praise you because...
Confession: Admit your sins and ask for forgiveness. 1 John 1:9, Psalm 139:23-24	Idolatry (worshipping something above God), Anger, Covetousness, Sexual Immorality, Lust, Pride, Vengeance, Hate, Drunkenness, Slander, Unforgiveness, Murder, Stealing, Selfishness, Lying, Greed, Hardness of Heart, etc.	Father, please forgive me for...
Thanksgiving: Thank God for what He is doing and the gifts that He gives. Psalm 136, James 1:17	Jesus, Holy Spirit, Blessings, Redemption, Peace, Joy, Purpose, Answered prayers, Wisdom, Discipline, Trials, Comfort, Strength, Scripture, Provisions, Freedom in Christ, etc.	Father, thank you for...
Supplication: Make your requests to God for yourself and for others. 1 Timothy 2:1-4, Phil. 4:6-7	Our spiritual growth, God's Kingdom's growth, God's glory growth, Provisions, Blessings, Healing, Deliverance, Guidance, Work, Fruit of the Spirit (Gal. 5), etc.	God, please help me... God, I pray for _____, that you would...

S.O.A.P.	BIBLE READING TOOL : EXAMPLE
Scripture - As you read, highlight verses, words, phrases that jump out to you. Write out any key verse(s).	Matthew 6:31-33: "So do not worry, saying, 'What shall we eat?' or 'What shall we drink?' or 'What shall we wear?' For the pagans run after all these things, and your heavenly Father knows that you need them. But seek first his kingdom and his righteousness, and all these things will be given to you as well."
Observation - Take note of what happened in the passage. Is there a theme or lesson? Did you learn anything about God?	Jesus is speaking and says, "Do not worry." "Pagan" means non-Christian. My Heavenly Father knows what I need. Seek God's kingdom and righteousness first and all these things will be given as well. He promises to provide for me, but He doesn't promise it will be how or when I want.
Application - Ask God to show you how to apply this passage to your life. Maybe there is something for you to learn, change, do, or just grow in wisdom and knowledge of who God is.	Pagans worry because they don't believe in God so they feel like everything is up to themselves or chance, but I don't have to carry that weight because I am a child of God and He knows my needs. Not only does He know my needs, but He promises to provide them, which is possible because all power and resources belong to Him. My worrying doesn't help anything, so stop letting worry ruin my mood and days. *Turn worrisome thoughts into prayers and then walk in peace and trust.* In the good, hard, and busy, continue seeking God FIRST in my day and FIRST in my heart!
Prayer ⟶	End in prayer by thanking God for His presence with you and enlightenment in this time. Pray for the indwelling Holy Spirit's help to carry out any application from God's Word.

APPLY S.O.A.P. TO COLOSSIANS:
Check off a box each day

- ☐ Col. 1:1-8
- ☐ Col. 1:9-14
- ☐ Col. 1: 15-23
- ☐ Col. 1:24-29
- ☐ Col. 2:1-15
- ☐ Col. 2:16-23
- ☐ Col. 3:1-11
- ☐ Col. 3:12-4:1
- ☐ Col. 4:2-6
- ☐ Col. 4:7-18

"

Let God's promises shine on
your problems.
-Corrie ten Boom

"

Today, I'm thankful for:

1. ....

2. ....

3. ....

PRAYING CLOSE:

Thoughts + Dreams:

Something I'm looking
forward to today is:

PRAYING FAR:

Verse

> " To him who is able to keep you from stumbling and to present you before his glorious presence without fault and with great joy— to the only God our Savior be glory, majesty, power and authority, through Jesus Christ our Lord, before all ages, now and forevermore! Amen.
> -Jude 24-25

TODAY'S PRIORITIES:

Today, I'm thankful for:

1. ....

2. ....

3. ....

PRAYING CLOSE:

Thoughts + Dreams:

Something I'm looking forward to today is:

PRAYING FAR:

Verse

"

Anything is a blessing that
makes us pray.
-Charles Spurgeon

"

Today, I'm thankful for:

1. ....
2. ....
3. ....

PRAYING CLOSE:

Thoughts + Dreams:

Something I'm looking
forward to today is:

PRAYING FAR:

Verse

There would be no sense in saying
you trusted Jesus if you would not
take his advice.
-C.S. Lewis

TODAY'S PRIORITIES:

Today, I'm thankful for:

1. ....

2. ....

3. ....

PRAYING CLOSE:

Thoughts + Dreams:

*Something I'm looking
forward to today is:*

PRAYING FAR:

Verse

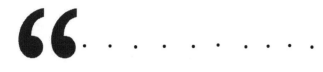

Enter his gates with thanksgiving
and his courts with praise; give
thanks to him and praise his name.
-Psalm 100:4

TODAY'S PRIORITIES:

Today, I'm thankful for:

1. ....

2. ....

3. ....

PRAYING CLOSE:

Thoughts + Dreams:

*Something I'm looking
forward to today is:*

PRAYING FAR:

Verse

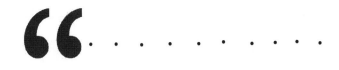

There is no pit so deep, that
God's love is not deeper still.
-Corrie ten Boom

TODAY'S PRIORITIES:

Today, I'm thankful for:

1. ....

2. ....

3. ....

PRAYING CLOSE:

Thoughts + Dreams:

*Something I'm looking
forward to today is:*

PRAYING FAR:

Verse

Reflect on this past year. Try to recall any significant things or themes God has been revealing to you. They could be characteristics or promises of God, or they could be things He has revealed about you. Then draw an image that captures that "revelation" and write out a verse that goes along with it.

(For example, this past year God has revealed to me that the pressure I put on myself to have everyone like me and "approve" of me is draining and debilitating. He reminded me that my identity is in CHRIST, and my life is with Him and for Him- not for the praise of others. This has brought me so much freedom in so many areas, so I would draw a bird flying out of a cage to capture this breakthrough lesson. I would also write out the verse 2 Corinthians 3:17.)

draw below

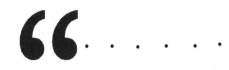

Is anyone among you in trouble? Let them pray. Is anyone happy? Let them sing songs of praise.
-James 5:13

TODAY'S PRIORITIES:

Today, I'm thankful for:

1. ....

2. ....

3. ....

PRAYING CLOSE:

Thoughts + Dreams:

Something I'm looking forward to today is:

PRAYING FAR:

Verse

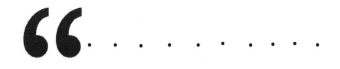

> To be a Christian means to forgive the inexcusable, because God has forgiven the inexcusable in you.
> -C.S. Lewis

TODAY'S PRIORITIES:

Today, I'm thankful for:

1. ....

2. ....

3. ....

PRAYING CLOSE:

Thoughts + Dreams:

Something I'm looking forward to today is:

PRAYING FAR:

Verse

> **"** But he said to me, My grace is suffi-
> cient for you, for my power is made
> perfect in weakness. Therefore I will
> boast all the more gladly about my
> weaknesses, so that Christ's power
> may rest on me.
> -2 Corinthians 12:9 **"**

TODAY'S PRIORITIES:

Today, I'm thankful for:

1. ....

2. ....

3. ....

PRAYING CLOSE:

Thoughts + Dreams:

*Something I'm looking
forward to today is:*

PRAYING FAR:

Verse

> I am the vine, you are the branches; he who abides in Me and I in him, he bears much fruit, for apart from Me you can do nothing.
> -John 15:4-5

TODAY'S PRIORITIES:

Today, I'm thankful for:

1. ....

2. ....

3. ....

PRAYING CLOSE:

Thoughts + Dreams:

Something I'm looking forward to today is:

PRAYING FAR:

Verse

But the fruit of the Spirit is love, joy, peace, patience, kindness, goodness, faithfulness, gentleness, and self-control.
-Galations 5:22-23

TODAY'S PRIORITIES:

Today, I'm thankful for:

1. ....

2. ....

3. ....

PRAYING CLOSE:

Thoughts + Dreams:

Something I'm looking forward to today is:

PRAYING FAR:

Verse

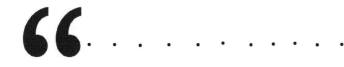

TODAY'S PRIORITIES:

Is prayer your steering wheel
or your spare tire?
-Corrie ten Boom

Today, I'm thankful for:

1. ....

2. ....

3. ....

PRAYING CLOSE:

Thoughts + Dreams:

*Something I'm looking
forward to today is:*

PRAYING FAR:

Verse

Happy Thoughts

What book has had a positive impact on your life? How so?

What movie has had a positive impact on your life? How so?

What song(s) impacted you positively? How so?

Write about a scent that takes you back to a happy memory?

What are two things that make you happy to see?

1

2

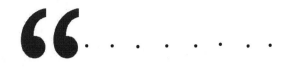

Be the reason someone believes in the goodness of God.

TODAY'S PRIORITIES:

Today, I'm thankful for:

1. ....

2. ....

3. ....

PRAYING CLOSE:

Thoughts + Dreams:

Something I'm looking forward to today is:

PRAYING FAR:

Verse

"

Rejoice in the Lord always. I
will say it again: Rejoice!
-Philippians 4:4

"

Today, I'm thankful for:

1. ....

2. ....

3. ....

PRAYING CLOSE:

Thoughts + Dreams:

*Something I'm looking
forward to today is:*

PRAYING FAR:

Verse

> *I waited patiently for the Lord; he turned to me and heard my cry. He lifted me out of the slimy pit, out of the mud and mire; he set my feet on a rock and gave me a firm place to stand. He put a new song in my mouth, a hymn of praise to our God.*
> *-Psalm 40:1-3*

TODAY'S PRIORITIES:

Today, I'm thankful for:

1. ....

2. ....

3. ....

PRAYING CLOSE:

Thoughts + Dreams:

Something I'm looking forward to today is:

PRAYING FAR:

Verse

> "
> God whispers to us in our pleasures,
> speaks in our conscience, but shouts in
> our pains: it is his megaphone to rouse a
> deaf world.
> -C.S. Lewis
> "

Today, I'm thankful for:

1. ....

2. ....

3. ....

PRAYING CLOSE:

Thoughts + Dreams:

Something I'm looking
forward to today is:

PRAYING FAR:

Verse

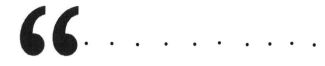

Look to the Lord and his
strength; seek his face
always.
-1 Chronicles 16:11

TODAY'S PRIORITIES:

Today, I'm thankful for:

1. ....

2. ....

3. ....

PRAYING CLOSE:

Thoughts + Dreams:

*Something I'm looking
forward to today is:*

PRAYING FAR:

Verse

> Therefore, my beloved brothers, be steadfast, immovable, always abounding in the work of the Lord, knowing that in the Lord your labor is not in vain.
> -1 Corinthians 5:58

Today, I'm thankful for:

1. ....

2. ....

3. ....

PRAYING CLOSE:

Thoughts + Dreams:

Something I'm looking forward to today is:

PRAYING FAR:

Verse

Have you ever wondered how you can grow your relationship with God? It's actually pretty simple!

Check out the wheel picture on the next page. Read how the 4 spokes reflect 4 different ways that we can grow in our relationship with God.

~~~~~~

Which of the spokes do you feel like you thrive in the most?

Why do you think that may be?

Which of the spokes do you feel like you neglect the most?

Why do you think that may be?

Considering these 4 spokes, what are some possible steps you could take to grow in your relationship with God?

SPIRITUAL HEALTH

Navigator
Discipleship
Tool

THE WHEEL

The Wheel diagram, created by Navigator founder Dawson Trotman in the 1930s, is a simple, effective way to visually explain the structure of a God-glorifying life. Sharing it can be as simple as drawing it on a napkin or notepad. The diagram challenges us to think deeply about how to be an obedient follower of Christ as each part represents a crucial component of a vibrant Christian life.

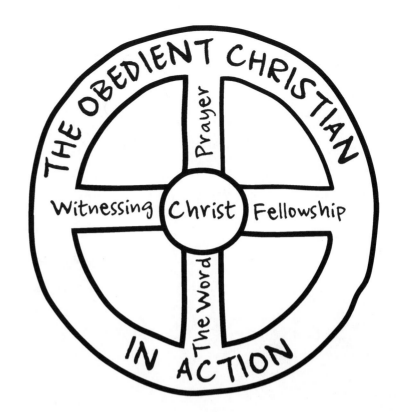

How you relate to yourself
THE VOLITIONAL DIMENSION

The Hub: Christ the Center: Total surrender to Christ's authority and lordship is not always a decision made right at conversion, but is a necessary act of will. For the believer, the "old life" has gone and the new has come (2 Corinthians 5:17), and Christ dwells through us instead (Galatians 2:20). God creates within us the desire to do what He wants us to do in order to express His lordship in our lives.

• **The Rim**: Obedience to Christ: Some acts of obedience to God are internal, such as attitudes, habits, motives, values and day-to-day thoughts. But even these eventually surface outwardly in our relationships with other people. Keeping His commandments in obedience is our outward indication of inward health and love for Christ-our worship (John 14:21, Romans 12:1).

How you relate to God.
THE VERTICAL DIMENSION

• **The Word Spoke**: The Word of God is His direct voice showing us not only who He is, but how to live and interact with everyone around us (2 Timothy 3:16). This means an earnest personal intake of God's Word is essential for health and growth (Joshua 1:8). As God speaks to us through the Scriptures, we can see His principles for life and ministry, learn how to obey Him and become acquainted with the Christ who is worthy of our steadfast allegiance.

• **The Prayer Spoke**: Prayer is the natural response to God as we hear Him speak through His Word. It is sharing our heart with the One who longs for our companionship and who cares about our concerns. Prayer not only trains our hearts and minds to know the power and glory of God, but also turns His ear towards action in our lives and of those who we pray for (John 15:7, Philippians 4:6-7).

How you relate to others.
THE HORIZONTAL DIMENSION

• **The Word Spoke**: The Word of God is His direct voice showing us not only who He is, but how to live and interact with everyone around us (2 Timothy 3:16). This means an earnest personal intake of God's Word is essential for health and growth (Joshua 1:8). As God speaks to us through the Scriptures, we can see His principles for life and ministry, learn how to obey Him and become acquainted with the Christ who is worthy of our steadfast allegiance.

• **The Prayer Spoke**: Prayer is the natural response to God as we hear Him speak through His Word. It is sharing our heart with the One who longs for our companionship and who cares about our concerns. Prayer not only trains our hearts and minds to know the power and glory of God, but also turns His ear towards action in our lives and of those who we pray for (John 15:7, Philippians 4:6-7).

> Fear not, for I am with you; be not dismayed, for I am your God; I will strengthen you, I will help you, I will uphold you with my righteous right hand.
> -Isaiah 41:10

TODAY'S PRIORITIES:

Today, I'm thankful for:

1. ....

2. ....

3. ....

PRAYING CLOSE:

Thoughts + Dreams:

Something I'm looking forward to today is:

PRAYING FAR:

Verse

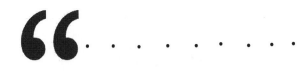

God has given us two hands, one to receive with and the other to give with.
-Billy Graham

Today, I'm thankful for:

1. ....

2. ....

3. ....

PRAYING CLOSE:

Thoughts + Dreams:

Something I'm looking forward to today is:

PRAYING FAR:

Verse

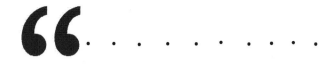

For freedom Christ has set us
free; stand firm therefore, and
do not submit again to a yoke of
slavery.
-Galations 5:1

TODAY'S PRIORITIES:

Today, I'm thankful for:

1. ....

2. ....

3. ....

PRAYING CLOSE:

Thoughts + Dreams:

*Something I'm looking
forward to today is:*

PRAYING FAR:

Verse

> Come to me, all who labor and are
> heavy laden, and I will give you rest.
> Take my yoke upon you, and learn from
> me, for I am gentle and lowly in heart,
> and you will find rest for your souls.
> -Matthew 11:28-30

TODAY'S PRIORITIES:

Today, I'm thankful for:

1. ....

2. ....

3. ....

PRAYING CLOSE:

Thoughts + Dreams:

Something I'm looking forward to today is:

PRAYING FAR:

Verse

> Trust in the Lord with all your heart, and do not lean on your own understanding. In all your ways acknowledge him, and he will make straight your paths.
> -Proverbs 3:5-6

TODAY'S PRIORITIES:

Today, I'm thankful for:

1. ....

2. ....

3. ....

PRAYING CLOSE:

Thoughts + Dreams:

Something I'm looking forward to today is:

PRAYING FAR:

Verse

"

My home is in Heaven. I'm just
traveling through this world.
-Billy Graham

"

Today, I'm thankful for:

1. ....

2. ....

3. ....

PRAYING CLOSE:

Thoughts + Dreams:

*Something I'm looking
forward to today is:*

PRAYING FAR:

Verse

Hebrews 13:5 says, "Keep your lives free from the love of money and be content with what you have, because God has said, 'Never will I leave you; never will I forsake you.'"

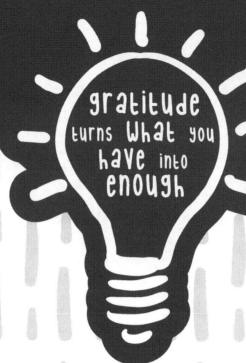

gratitude turns what you have into enough

Name something in every room of your house that you are thankful for and why:

" · · · · · · · · · · · · · · ·

So then, just as you received Christ Jesus as Lord, continue to live your lives in him, rooted and built up in him, strengthened in the faith as you were taught, and overflowing with thankfulness.
-Colossians 2:6-7

· · · · · · · · · · · · · · "

TODAY'S PRIORITIES:

Today, I'm thankful for:

1. ....

2. ....

3. ....

PRAYING CLOSE:

Thoughts + Dreams:

Something I'm looking forward to today is:

PRAYING FAR:

Verse

> Whatever happens, conduct your-
> selves in a manner worthy of the
> gospel of Christ.
> -Philippians 1:27

TODAY'S PRIORITIES:

Today, I'm thankful for:

1. ....

2. ....

3. ....

PRAYING CLOSE:

Thoughts + Dreams:

*Something I'm looking
forward to today is:*

PRAYING FAR:

Verse

> God allows us to experience the low points of life in order to teach us lessons that we could learn in no other way.
> -C.S. Lewis

TODAY'S PRIORITIES:

Today, I'm thankful for:

1. ....

2. ....

3. ....

PRAYING CLOSE:

Thoughts + Dreams:

Something I'm looking forward to today is:

PRAYING FAR:

Verse

> For our struggle is not against flesh and blood, but against the rulers, against the authorities, against the powers of this dark world and against the spiritual forces of evil in the heavenly realms. Therefore put on the full armor of God...
> -Ephesians 6:10-13

TODAY'S PRIORITIES:

Today, I'm thankful for:

1. ....

2. ....

3. ....

PRAYING CLOSE:

Thoughts + Dreams:

Something I'm looking forward to today is:

PRAYING FAR:

Verse

"

But now he has reconciled you by Christ's physical body through death to present you holy in his sight, without blemish and free from accusation— if you continue in your faith, established and firm, and do not move from the hope held out in the gospel.
-Colossians 1:22-23

"

Today, I'm thankful for:

1. ....

2. ....

3. ....

PRAYING CLOSE:

Thoughts + Dreams:

Something I'm looking forward to today is:

PRAYING FAR:

Verse

> " Love is patient, love is kind. It does not envy, it does not boast, it is not proud. It does not dishonor others, it is not self-seeking, it is not easily angered, it keeps no record of wrongs. Love does not delight in evil but rejoices with the truth. It always protects, always trusts, always hopes, always perseveres. Love never fails. "
> -1 Corinthians 13:4-8

TODAY'S PRIORITIES:

Today, I'm thankful for:

1. ....

2. ....

3. ....

PRAYING CLOSE:

Thoughts + Dreams:

Something I'm looking forward to today is:

PRAYING FAR:

Verse

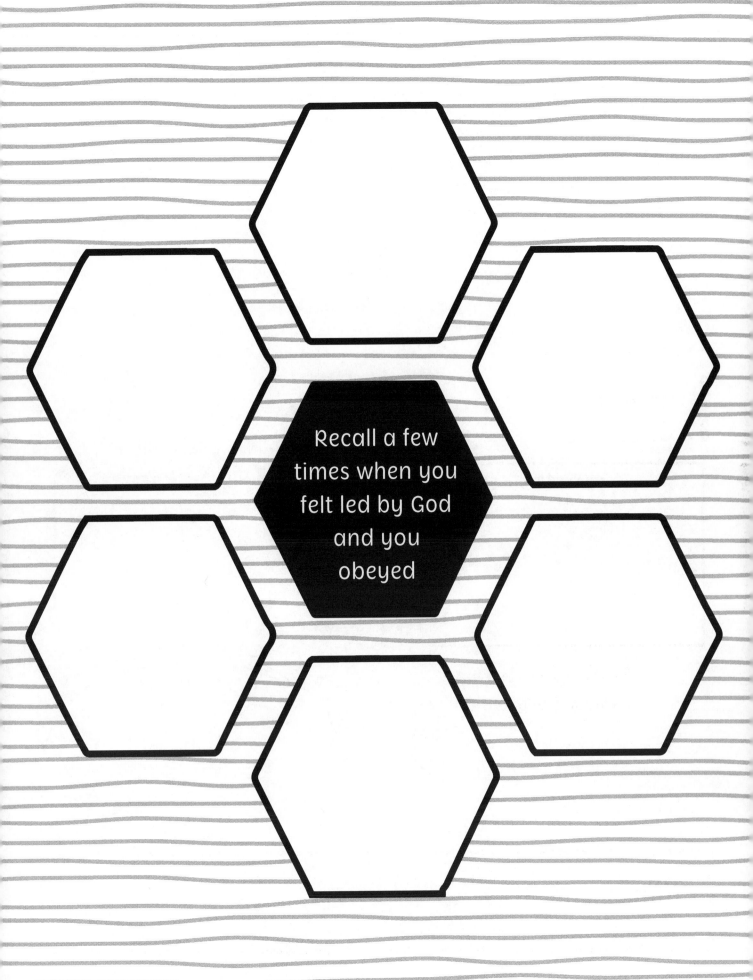

Recall a few times when you felt led by God and you obeyed

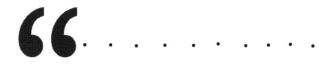

Now to him who is able to do im-
measurably more than all we ask
or imagine, according to his power
that is at work within us.
-Ephesians 3:20

TODAY'S PRIORITIES:

Today, I'm thankful for:

1. ....

2. ....

3. ....

PRAYING CLOSE:

Thoughts + Dreams:

Something I'm looking forward to today is:

PRAYING FAR:

Verse

"WHAT WE DO IN THIS SEASON MATTERS
WHAT WE SAY IN THIS SEASON MATTERS
WHAT WE PRAY IN THIS SEASON MATTERS
WHAT WE READ IN THIS SEASON MATTERS
WHAT WE WATCH IN THIS SEASON MATTERS
WHAT WE THINK IN THIS SEASON MATTERS
WHAT WE LEARN IN THIS SEASON MATTERS
WHAT WE RELEASE IN THIS SEASON MATTERS
WHAT WE BELIEVE IN THIS SEASON MATTERS

It may not always seem like it, but the day-to-day things matter.
God can work in and through every circumstance
to bring light, hope, fruit, and restoration."

-Christine Caine

NO SEASON IS
EVER WASTED

◆ Cut out to display or frame for encouragement ◆

"And should I ever need reminding of how I've been set free, there is a cross that bears the burden where another died for me.

And should I ever need reminding what power set me free, there is a grave that holds no body and now that power lives in me.

And should I ever need reminding how good you've been to me, I'll count the joy come every battle 'cause I know that's where you'll be."

– "Another in the Fire" by Hillsong

His Mercies Are New Every Morning

Discover more titles from Creative Ideas Publishing

  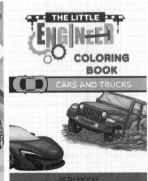 

Made in the USA
Columbia, SC
20 November 2020